Compass Point Books
1710 Roe Crest Drive
North Mankato, MN 56003

Editor: Jeni Wittrock
Designer: Sarah Bennett
Media Researcher: Marcie Spence
Production Specialists: Danielle Ceminsky

Acknowledgments
Special thanks to Arlee, Clay, and Betsy Twitchell, Luke McNaboe,
and Farmers Mark Palladino and Joanie Guglielmino, Wild Carrot Farm,
Canton, Connecticut, for sharing their stories with me.

 This book was manufactured with paper containing
at least 10 percent post-consumer waste.

Library of Congress Cataloging-in-Publication Data
Rau, Dana Meachen
Going organic: a healthy guide to making the switch/by Dana Meachen Rau.
    p. cm.
  Summary: "Describes the benefits, challenges, and steps to switching to an
organic diet"—Provided by publisher.
  Includes bibliographical references and index.
ISBN 978-0-7565-4523-9 (library binding)
ISBN 978-0-7565-4528-4 (paperback)
1. Health—Juvenile literature. 2. Natural foods—Juvenile literature.
3. Nutrition—Juvenile literature. I. Title.
  RA784.R382 2012
  613.2—dc23   4516   2011040704

Image Credits: Alamy Images: Ambient Images, Inc., 9, Andrew Rubtsov,
41, Jeff Greenberg, 10 (top), MarioPonta, 35, Nathan Luke, 56; AP Images:
Hartford Courant, Stephen Dunn, 54-55; Capstone Studio: Karon Dubke,
cover, 11, 23, 26-27, 32, 33, 47, 59; Corbis: Brooks Kraft, 51, Oren Rosenfeld/
Demotix, 19; Getty Images: Larry Dale Gordon, 5; Shutterstock: Aaron Amat,
53, Alaettin Yildirim, 16-17, Alison Hancock, 57 (bottom), Amy Myers, 25,
Benis Arapovic, 37 (top), Blend Images, 22 (left), Bull's-Eye Art, 21 (right),
Carly Rose Hennigan, 46, Charles Amundson, 38, Christi Tolbert, 7 (right),
Denis and Yulia Pogostins, 58, Denton Rumsey, 6-7, EcoPrint, 20-21, Elena
Elisseeva, 52, Emjay Smith, 14 (top), fusebulb, 17 (bottom), Ilya Akinshin, 14
(bottom), Ivonne Wlerink, 44, Jason Swarr, 30, Jason Winter, 36, 37 (bottom),
Liem Bahneman, 40, Matthew Jacques, 13, Monkey Business Images, 45,
Orange Line Media, 22 (right), Scruggelgreen, 49, SeDmi, 28, Sue McDonald,
10 (bottom), Tanis Saucier, 57 (top), Thoma, 16 (left), Tish1, 31, Tomo
Jesenicnik, 29, WimL, 18, Yellowj, 20 (left)

Visit Compass Point Books on the Internet at *www.capstonepub.com*.

Printed in the United States of America in North Mankato, Minnesota.
102011   006405CGS12

CONTENTS

CHAPTER ONE

POWER OF YOUR PLATE

WOULD YOU LIKE CEREAL OR EGGS FOR BREAKFAST?

How about soup or a sandwich for lunch? Dinner could be pasta with sauce or beans with rice. Our fridges and cabinets are stocked with a world of food choices.

Have you ever really thought about where all that food comes from? You might say "from a store." But food starts in ranches and farm fields. Some foods are even created in laboratories.

The world population is 7 billion. The United States alone is home to about 300 million of those people. Feeding everyone isn't easy. The food industry is a massive collection of farmers, ranchers, and manufacturers. Food often passes through many hands and machines before it makes its way to your grocery store and then to your plate.

Health-conscious people are concerned that some of our food has lost its natural qualities through this process. Plants and animals are sometimes given artificial substances to help them

Even the most carefully applied pesticides can be dangerous.

**Americans
Eat a Lot!**

In one year, the average
American ate:

DAIRY PRODUCTS
600.5 pounds

VEGETABLES
392.7 pounds

FRUIT
250.9 pounds

FLOUR & CEREAL PRODUCTS
196.5 pounds

RED MEAT
108.3 pounds

POULTRY
72.6 pounds

FISH AND SHELLFISH
16.0 pounds

EGGS
247 eggs

grow. Crops are sprayed with pesticides to keep away insects and weeds. Foods are enhanced with additives, fillers, and dyes.

So what's the problem? The chemicals used in the process of growing, raising, and processing foods make their way into our land, water, and air. And they make their way into you when you eat them. A growing number of farms, companies, and people like you have chosen to go organic.

You have the power to make a healthier world with every bite.

NURTURE NATURE

Luke has a lot going on. He fills his days with high school, homework, cross-country practice, a part-time job, and keeping up with friends. He also tends to his chickens.

In the mornings Luke lets the chickens out of the coop. The chickens forage in the backyard while Luke changes their water and collects the fresh eggs. At night he secures the chickens in their coop again. Once a week he gives them fresh pellets to eat. Every two weeks he cleans and stocks the coop with fresh hay.

Thanks to the chickens, Luke's family enjoys a lot of fresh eggs. Sometimes they even have enough to sell to friends and neighbors.

Organic foods, like Luke's backyard eggs, are grown and processed in a more natural way to help conserve the health of land, animals, and crops. Like Luke, many kids and teens are playing an active part in controlling where their food comes from. Are you thinking of going organic too?

Backyard gardens and chicken coops are just one way you can take your food into your own hands. You may not have the space, time, or best location to grow or raise your own food. But you can do your best to seek out organic food where you live.

You Have It Easy!

Access to a variety of foods wasn't always so easy. Native Americans and early settlers hunted, gathered, and grew their own food. Farmers withstood backbreaking labor, insects, drought, and long, lean winters.

Innovations throughout history made food-making a whole lot easier. Better equipment and farming methods cut down on work. Refrigeration kept food fresh. Transportation brought regional foods to more people. Grocery stores offered packed shelves. Restaurants shared international flavors.

Thanks to these steps in the food industry, we have many choices today.

Backyard chicken coops let you collect organic eggs at home.

Next time you're in a grocery store, you may see bunches of organic lettuce next to the regular lettuce. In the dairy aisle, organic yogurt and regular yogurt may sit side by side. Your store may even have a whole aisle devoted to organic packaged foods. As you drive around town, you might notice farm stands and markets brimming baskets of corn or peppers. You may even see signs for the grand opening of an all-organic grocery store.

According to NOP regulations, organic means:

CROPS
- are not grown with synthetic pesticides
- are not grown with synthetic or sewage sludge-based fertilizers
- are not grown from genetically engineered seeds
- are not irradiated to kill bacteria

ANIMALS
- are fed organic feed (with no animal by-products)
- are given access to the outdoors
- are not given growth hormones
- are not given antibiotics
- are not irradiated to kill bacteria

PACKAGED FOODS
- cannot use genetically modified organisms (GMOs), irradiation, artificial dyes, or preservatives
- must be protected from contamination
- cannot have packaging material that contains fungicides, preservatives, or fumigants
- must use approved labels

Farmers markets can be a great source for organic foods.

Small farms and large companies across the country are going organic. The United States Department of Agriculture (USDA) has established a National Organic Program (NOP) with standards that define organic products. If a farm or company follows the guidelines, it can place an official "organic" label on its produce, meat, or packaged foods. That makes it easier for you, the customer, to know more about where your food comes from.

THE ULTIMATE OMELET

Whether your raise your own chickens or buy organic eggs, an omelet makes an ultimate meal—for breakfast, lunch, or dinner!

Ingredients*

2 large eggs

1 teaspoon butter

fresh chives, chopped

¼ cup cubed ham

1 ½ ounces grated
   cheddar cheese

salt and pepper to taste

** Look for organic versions
   of these ingredients
   when possible.*

Steps

Break the eggs into a small bowl and whisk to combine.

Place the butter in a small skillet. Heat on the stove on medium high until the butter melts.

Pour in the eggs. As they cook, lift up edges with a turner to let the wet, uncooked eggs on top reach the hot pan below.

When the eggs are almost cooked through, sprinkle the eggs with chives, ham, and cheese.

Fold the omelet in half with the turner. Let it cook another minute.

Slide it onto a plate. Season with salt and pepper.

WHY ORGANIC?

FROM THE TIME YOU WERE LITTLE, picture books and television shows have portrayed farmers in overalls, cows grazing on grass, and wheat waving in fields. E-I-E-I-O.

Idealistic family farms still exist across the country, but most of our food comes from much larger farms that work like factories. Like any company, a farm tries to run efficiently—which means churning out the most products for the least amount of money.

But what's the real cost of processing food this way? We pay a heavy toll for processed foods, and one important cost is measured in more than dollars.

Farmers use animal manure to add nutrients back into the soil.

Fertilizers and pesticides can seep into sources of drinking water.

CROPS ON A CONVENTIONAL FARM

In fields you see the tops of the plants standing tall to reach the sun. But deep underground, their roots suck up the soil's nutrients. What happens after a crop has used all the good plant food in the soil? Farmers have to put it back in for the next round of crops. On conventional farms, they do this by adding chemical fertilizers or manure produced by their animals.

They also use pesticides, including insecticides, to help fight the battles against hungry insects that can destroy crops. They might treat their fields with herbicides or fungicides to combat weeds and fungi.

So what's the cost to the environment? While a chemical fertilizer may help a plant grow, over time it strips the land of nutrients. Fertilizers and pesticides seep into the groundwater.

That means they can harm the wildlife in nearby streams or make their way into your sources of drinking water. Insecticides sometimes kill more than just the bad bugs. They may kill the beneficial ones too. They may also harm or kill birds or small animals that feed on insects.

Farmers may also use genetically engineered seeds. Scientists have altered the DNA of these seeds to give the plants an advantage, such as stronger stalks or resistance to insects. But the science of genetically modifying seeds is a new technology. There hasn't been time to watch the long-term effects of messing with Mother Nature.

The Dirty Dozen

The Environmental Working Group, a nonprofit research organization based in Washington, D.C., gathered pesticide data and created a list it calls the "Dirty Dozen." Because of the way these fruits and vegetables grow and their susceptibility to insects, they tend to have high pesticide levels if grown on conventional farms.

If you decide to go organic, these might be the best products to switch first:

apples

lettuce

peaches

bell peppers

grapes
[imported]

potatoes

blueberries
[domestic]

kale/collard
greens

spinach

strawberries

celery

nectarines
[domestic]

ANIMALS ON A CAFO

Animals for most of our meat products are raised on large, factory-like farms called concentrated animal feeding operations (CAFOs). On CAFOs farmers can feed and raise hundreds or thousands of animals at once. Cows are kept in tightly-packed pens called feedlots. Chickens crowd the floor of chicken sheds.

Cows raised create a lot of feces. Because there's not much room to roam in crowded feedlots, the waste piles deeper and deeper. Some cows spend much of their lives in this waste.

Ammonia, hydrogen sulfide, and methane are three dangerous chemicals found in the gases emitted from CAFO waste.

Infections can spread easily in the crowded conditions of CAFOs (concentrated animal feeding operations).

Some waste gets on the animals' fur. When they are slaughtered, some of the feces might get on their meat. E. coli is a very dangerous, deadly bacteria found in waste. If it gets in people's food, it leads to extreme illness or death. Farmers have to irradiate meat to kill harmful bacteria by exposing it to light rays.

Infections also spread easily in crowded conditions. You probably know that from school—when one person gets sick, many others in your class get sick too. Antibiotics stop bacterial infections before they spread. So farmers give their animals antibiotics.

Farmers also give animals doses of antibiotics to kill disease-causing bacteria related to what they eat. The animals aren't always fed their natural diets. Animal feed sometimes contains animal by-products, such as chicken feathers or feces, or the scrap parts of pigs, horses, and chickens. A cow's body is built to digest grass. But at feedlots they are fed corn. Since this is unnatural for them, they can get sick.

Farmers may also use growth hormones, which make animals grow to maturity faster. If it takes less time for the animal to grow,

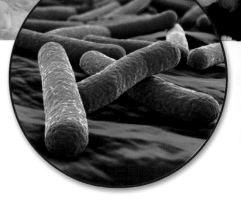

E. coli bacteria is found in animal feces. It can be deadly.

the farmer will be able to produce more meat. Hormones are also given to dairy cows so they will produce more milk.

If animals are given antibiotics or hormones, traces of those substances come out in their waste. If the waste is used as manure to fertilize crops, the antibiotics and hormones can get into the soil and then into the plants that grow in it.

The substances that go into growing and raising your food make their way into the food. And that means they make their way into *you*.

FRIENDLY FARMS

The mission of an organic farm is to return to a more natural way of farming. Farmers who follow the USDA's National Organic Program regulations strive to reduce pollution of the land, water, and air. These farmers try to improve the quality of the soil and the health of their animals.

Instead of chemical fertilizers, organic farmers let the plants do the work. Farmers rotate their crops, which means they don't plant the same crop on the same field season after season. Some plants help put nutrients back into the soil, and some take them away. Farmers try to find the right balance to keep the soil healthy. Organic farmers may also put composted plant scraps and manure in the soil to add nutrients.

Once farmers plant crops in healthy soil, they need to protect them. Their next challenge is to fight the battle of the bugs and weeds. Instead of insecticides, farmers might rely on natural insect predators—such as birds or "good" insects. To avoid using herbicides, farmers might control weeds by covering areas with

Some farmers choose to weed crops by hand. Others use approved organic pesticides, such as vinegar, clove oil, and corn gluten meal.

mulch, weeding by hand, or tilling the field more often. They may choose to use an approved organic pesticide.

Organic farmers also monitor what's in their animals' feed. To be organic, feed has to be made of grains or other products that are grown organically (without pesticides or genetically modified seeds). The feed also can't contain any animal by-products.

The National Organic Program regulations require that animals be given access to the outdoors. While some organic farms still have crowded conditions, it is common organic practice to reduce the animals' stress. Chickens may be allowed to roam and peck. Pigs may wallow in mud. Cows may graze in pastures.

Battle of the Bugs

Lovely dotted ladybugs—they look so small and innocent. Ladybugs may be cute, but they are carnivores. Farmers like these beneficial insects because they devour the insects that destroy their crops. Farmers either rely on the native population of beneficial insects in the area, or purchase the insects and introduce them to their fields. This is called biocontrol—using natural enemies to control pests instead of chemical pesticides.

If a newly introduced or invasive species kills off another species, however, the balance of the food chain in that ecosystem could be affected. To avoid this problem, a farmer might instead encourage the presence of an existing population of beneficial insects by planting flowers or other crops that attract them to an area.

Organic farmers who allow their cows to graze solve more than one problem. They rotate their cows among different pastures. The cows have more room to roam, get to eat grass, and "mow" the grass for the farmer. When the cows move to a new pasture, the grass has time to grow back, providing a continuous food supply. A grass diet for cows reduces the risk of disease, so farmers don't need to use antibiotics or irradiation. Manure falls to the ground as the cows eat, which fertilizes the soil to keep it healthy and helps the grass grow back.

Organic farmers try to reduce animal stress through practices such as allowing cows to graze in pastures.

ORGANIC, SUSTAINABLE, LOCAL—WHAT'S THE DIFFERENCE?

You might hear the word "organic" paired with "sustainable" and "local." While the meanings of these terms often overlap, there are differences among them.

Sustainable means farmers replace what they take from the land so they don't use up an area's resources. They respect the environment by avoiding excess waste, pollution, or damage. They look for ways to reduce transportation or processing energy. They respect their animals and pay their workers fairly. Communities can benefit from sustainable practices because some farmers sell

How Far Is Local?

Eating local can present some problems. What happens when you live in a city? And how do you eat local produce in the winter if you live where the ground gets covered in snow? Oranges grow in the South, so do northerners never get to eat oranges? What if the dry desert soil of your area can't produce many crops? Spices come from all over the world—cinnamon travels all the way from Indonesia. Does that mean no more cinnamon toast for you? As you can see, there are no clear answers to a lot of these questions. If you decide to "go local," know that you'll have to decide for yourself what local means to you.

You can find locally grown produce at a farmers market.

to them directly at farmers markets instead of grocery stores. Farming this way ensures a long, sustainable relationship between the farmer, the land, and his or her community.

You might notice bumper stickers that read "Eat Local." "Locavores" have decided to eat foods grown only within a certain radius of their home. For example, instead of buying a plum from Chile, you may be able to buy an apple or orange grown in your state. Eating local reduces the "food miles" a food has to travel from a farm to your plate. The more miles a food travels, the more energy is used to get it there. Often buying local also means food is fresher, ripened right on the vine. While the words have similarities, "sustainable" and "local" are not interchangeable with organic. A sustainable or local farm might still use pesticides. It might not feed its livestock organic grain. On the other hand, an organic tomato might have traveled thousands of miles to get to you.

So what's best? Organic, sustainable, or local? You have to decide for yourself. One solution can't solve all our environmental problems, but all of them are steps toward a healthier planet.

Let's Eat

GO GREEN GRASS-FED BEEF BURGER

You can't get much "greener" than grass. Enjoy the natural taste of open-pasture beef smothered with even more green goodness!

Ingredients*

1 pound grass-fed organic beef

crusty rolls

avocados, sliced

bean sprouts

fresh spinach

cucumbers, sliced

Steps

Form the beef into four patties.

Place on a hot grill and cook about 5 minutes on each side, or until the centers are no longer pink.

Place a burger on each roll, and top with avocado, sprouts, spinach, and cucumber. (Or any other green vegetable you like!)

* Look for organic versions of these ingredients when possible.

CHAPTER THREE

BODY BASICS

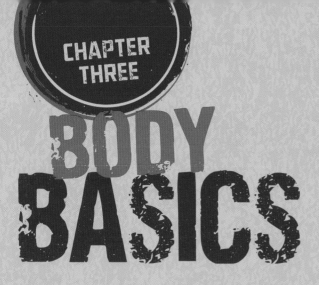

YOU ARE A WELL-OILED MACHINE. If you could get a factory tour of your body, you'd see blood rushing to deliver nutrients. You'd see muscles doing the power work, lifting, blinking, and swallowing. You'd watch cells battle to protect you against disease.

Eating a balanced diet gives your body what it needs. But have you ever thought about what it really, truly needs? You know what you like—maybe pizza, salad, and ice cream for dinner sound good to you. But how does your body use those foods to function? If you're taking the time to get to know where your food comes from, take the time to get to know your body.

MEANINGFUL MEALS

Your body gets five basic substances from food: carbohydrates, proteins, fats, vitamins, and minerals. Meaningful meals combine more than one of these categories.

The millions of cells in your body need carbohydrates—starches and sugars. Grains, such as wheat, oats, corn, and rice, are sources of carbohydrates. Fruit is filled with natural sugar. Your cells turn these carbohydrates into energy.

Protein builds your muscles and other body tissues. Lean meats, fish, eggs, beans, and nuts all contain valuable protein.

So do dairy foods, such as milk, yogurt, and cheese.

Fat is your body's spare energy source. You don't need a lot of fat in your diet, and saturated fat, trans fats, and cholesterol can be bad for you. But your body does need some fat. Get it from healthy sources, such as avocados, nuts, and fish.

Vitamins and minerals are vital for your body too. And you need them from a variety of sources. You can munch almonds to get vitamin E, the substance that helps your immune system. Leafy green vegetables and red meat contain iron, a mineral your body needs to help bring oxygen to your cells. Milk and other dairy products are good sources of calcium, which builds and grows your bones. A long list of vitamins and minerals have important tasks to help you function at your best.

IS ORGANIC BETTER FOR YOU?

We know that organic foods are better for the environment. But are they better for you?

The USDA does not officially state that organic foods are more healthful than conventional foods. And scientists have differing opinions on the advantage of organic versus conventional foods. But some studies have documented the benefits of going organic. Plant-based organic foods, such as produce and grains, have been proven to have higher levels of some nutrients, especially antioxidants that help your immune system.

Eating organic is safer for you too. Traces of pesticides remain on fruit

Eating in Season

To get the freshest organic food, it helps to eat produce that is in season in your area of the country. So when does the following popular produce grow where you live?

Region	Grapes	Strawberries	Watermelon	Broccoli	Lettuce	Peas
Northeast	Sept.–Oct.	June	Aug.–Oct.	June–Nov.	May–Oct.	July–Oct.
South	Aug.–Oct.	April–June	June–Aug.	April–May	fall–spring	July–Aug.
Southwest	July–Aug.	Feb.–April	July–Aug.	Oct.–March	Oct.–May	April–June
Midwest	Aug.–Sept.	June–July	Aug.–Sept.	June–Oct.	May–Oct.	June–Aug.
Upper Midwest	Sept.	June–July	Aug.–Sept.	June–Oct.	June–Sept.	July–Aug.
Northwest	Aug.–Oct.	June–July	Aug.–Sept.	June–Sept.	May–Nov.	June–July

and vegetables. Rinsing them, and even peeling them, doesn't necessarily get all the chemicals off. Pesticides have been linked to diseases and disorders, especially in children. And while crops are tested to make sure pesticide levels are safe, why subject your body to unnecessary chemicals?

Organic meats also help reduce your risk of eating harmful bacteria, such as E. coli or salmonella. Studies have also shown that grass-fed beef is low in fat and high in omega-3 fatty acids that are good for your heart.

Organic farms allow plants and animals to grow and eat more naturally to keep the earth healthy.

There are also benefits to living in a healthy environment with reduced pollution and waste. If you live near an organic farm, you shouldn't have to worry about contaminated drinking water. If organic is good for the earth, it's good for you. Fish swimming in clear rivers, animals eating in a balanced food chain, and crops soaking in the sun from a clean sky—they all thrive in a healthy environment. And you do too.

Prepackaged

Do you find it hard to give up overly packaged foods? Here are some foods that come in their own "packaging!"

oranges   bananas

sunflower seeds

peanuts

CLOSE TO NATURE

Maybe you're ready to start feeding your hunger with organic food. But remember this before you switch: Junk food is junk food, whether it's labeled organic or not.

You can take a big, crunchy bite of an organic apple. That apple looks pretty much the same as it did when it was growing on the tree. Or you can rip open a foil packet of organic chewy apple snacks. They're molded into cute shapes, taste like jelly beans, and are easy to pop in your mouth. Which one is better for your body? They're both fruit, right?

Overly processed foods are not always the healthiest choice, even if they are organic. Think about how much energy went into making your food. To turn that apple into "apple snacks," energy was used to clean, slice, mush, heat, pour, and mold that apple into a new form. Energy was used to make the foil packet, plastic tray, or cardboard box they came in. Energy was used to run all the machines at a factory.

The apple that still looks like an apple is more healthful. The closer you get to a food's natural state, the more chance you have of benefiting from the vitamins, minerals, and other nutrients that food holds and your body craves. Remember, *fresh* organic food is best.

Let's Eat

FEED THE MACHINE PIZZA

Feed your body everything it needs in one meal. This pizza/buffalo wing combination includes carbohydrates, protein, vitamins, minerals, and even some fat—everything that keeps your machine running.

Ingredients*

olive oil

prepared pizza dough

½ cup canned tomato sauce

2 teaspoons hot sauce

½ cup crumbled blue cheese

1 cup grated mozzarella cheese

1 cup shredded cooked chicken

1 stalk celery, chopped

crushed red pepper

* Look for organic versions of these ingredients when possible.

Steps

Preheat the oven to 425°F.

Grease a cookie sheet with olive oil. Roll the pizza dough flat onto the cookie sheet.

In a small bowl, combine the tomato sauce with the hot sauce. Spread the sauce onto the dough, leaving about a 1-inch edge all around.

Sprinkle with the blue cheese, mozzarella, and cooked chicken.

Sprinkle on the celery. Add crushed red pepper to taste.

Bake for about 15 to 20 minutes or until crust is golden and cooked through in the middle.

SHOPPING STRATEGIES

GOING ORGANIC SOUNDS GREAT. BUT HOW DO YOU GET STARTED? Most likely the adults in your family are the shoppers. So your first mission will be to share with them the benefits of going organic. Do some research, decide why going organic is important to you, and then tell them all about it.

Going organic can be challenging. Your next mission will be to research the local area. Keep your eye out for places you can buy organic foods. What did you find?

Some neighborhood stores are well stocked with organic options. Rural areas may have organic farms. But many town grocery stores may not carry organic foods. Do a little more digging. You can always order prepared organic foods to be shipped to your door.

Another challenge besides finding organic food is the cost. In general organic food is more expensive than average food. That's because it costs more for farmers to raise and grow. Large commercial farms often qualify for government subsidies, while smaller organic farms do not. The work involved to more naturally grow a crop or tend to animals takes more labor. Organic seeds and animal feed are much more expensive.

> The American Cancer Society estimates that more than 34,000 cancer deaths in the U.S. in 2011 were caused by environmental pollutants and occupational exposures.

Know Your Labels

Food labels can be confusing. Commercials, advertisements, and packages may claim their food is "healthy" or "natural," but those labels aren't always accurate. To be labeled organic, however, a food has to meet strict qualifications that are checked and approved by USDA certifying agents.

- 100% Organic: all of the product's ingredients must be organic
- Organic: at least 95 percent of the ingredients are organic
- Made with Organic Ingredients: at least 70 percent of the ingredients are organic

OTHER LABELS YOU MAY SEE:
- Free Range or Cage Free: These labels are most often found on chicken and eggs. "Free range" means that the chickens have had access to the outdoors. "Cage free" means no cages. Keep in mind that this label can sometimes be misleading. Free-range chickens may

still spend most of their lives indoors, and cage-free chickens may still live in very crowded conditions.

- No Hormones: This means the animals grew without the aid of hormones.
- Grass Fed or Open Pasture: "Grass fed" means cows have been fed their natural diet of grass or hay. "Open pasture" means that the cow did its eating outdoors in a pasture.
- Natural: This generally means the product has little processing and no artificial ingredients or colors. This label can be very misleading and some people believe it needs stricter guidelines.

You may have to shop more often if you buy organic food. Organic foods sometimes spoil faster. That's because they haven't been filled with extra preservatives to increase their shelf life.

Are you up for the challenge? Your family has to decide for itself if buying organic food is an option. Perhaps you can eat organic just part of the year, when a fruit or vegetable is in season, or when organic items at the grocery store are on sale.

The Organic Trade Association's 2011 Organic Industry Survey reported that in 2010, supermarkets and other mass market retailers claimed about 54 percent of organic food sales.

It may be almost impossible to make the switch completely over to organic foods. Instead, start by replacing a few items at a time. Try the organic ketchup instead of the conventional ketchup. Or maybe decide that you will just eat organic produce, but not worry about packaged foods. Even small steps toward organic are better than none.

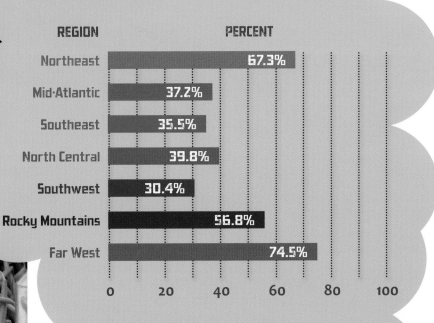

In a survey of farmers markets, the USDA found that organic products made up the following percent of their sales in 2005, the most recent year figures were available:

REGION	PERCENT
Northeast	67.3%
Mid-Atlantic	37.2%
Southeast	35.5%
North Central	39.8%
Southwest	30.4%
Rocky Mountains	56.8%
Far West	74.5%

0   20   40   60   80   100

FILLING YOUR BASKET

If you live in a rural area, take advantage of organic farms. Often they organize into farmers markets, where lots of vendors set up stalls—it's like an outdoor grocery store. Scan the newspaper or Internet for market schedules. In many communities they take place once a week through the growing season. Cities often hold farmers markets in an accessible, central location. Besides produce, farmers may also sell eggs, jams, honey, maple syrup, cheese, and other products. Many organic farms are approved by the USDA to be certified organic. But farms may still use organic practices without being certified. The advantage to shopping straight from farmers is that you can ask them yourself!

Farmers markets are well established in many cities around the United States.

More and more local grocery stores have organic food sections.

FILLING YOUR CART

If you don't have access to farms or farmers markets, you may be able to do all of your organic shopping at your local grocery store. As you walk down each aisle, look for the USDA Organic label. Do you see organic versions of the foods your family normally buys?

If the supermarket has a limited selection of organic foods, contact the store's customer service department. They'll direct you to the right person to ask about stocking more organic food. The store might not even know organic foods are in demand in their community.

At local restaurants, check the menu. They may feature foods with organic ingredients.

In addition to large grocery stores, towns and cities may also have smaller specialty stores. Look for natural food stores, organic grocery stores, butchers, bakeries, or produce markets too. Sometimes these stores have a variety of organic products, both fresh and packaged.

DINING OUT NATURALLY

You probably won't find organic meals at a fast food restaurant that churns out hundreds of hamburgers and fries a day. You may not be able to find organic ice cream when the ice cream truck drives by. But many restaurants have been turning to organic foods to foster a healthier planet and encourage a healthy lifestyle.

Some restaurants plan their entire menus around local organic produce and meats. They may even pull salad ingredients from their own backyard gardens. Other restaurants, while they might not be completely organic, will highlight organic items on their menus so you know a little more about where your dinner came from.

The National Restaurant Association's 2011 survey reports that 69 percent of adults say they are more likely to visit a restaurant that offers food grown or raised in an organic or environmentally-friendly way.

ON YOUR OWN

What kind of eater are you? Are you always on the go? You may want to look for organic foods that are quick and easy to grab or prepare, such as fruits, veggies, cereals, granola bars, or frozen dinners. Maybe you like to experiment in the kitchen. Look for fresh ingredients, wield your creative talents, and turn them into a satisfying meal for your whole family.

You can also become a small-scale farmer yourself from your window, porch, or backyard. A window box in a sunny window can hold plenty of herbs. You can grow tomatoes in a large pot. Find a sunny square in your yard, balcony, or patio, and get to work! When you're the farmer, you know your food's history, because you grew it yourself.

Fresh, organic produce gives creative cooks all kinds of options.

Grow Your Own!

Plants need three things to grow: Sunlight, soil, and water. That makes growing your own organic food easy.

Container gardens are small gardens you can grow in a pot instead of in the ground. Stop at a garden store or local farm and look for a deep pot, organic soil, and organic seeds. Herbs are good to start with. Try basil, oregano, rosemary, thyme, dill, or any other herb that looks appetizing and will grow well in your area.

Fill up your container with soil, leaving some room at the top, and follow the directions on the seed packet for how deep and far apart to place the seeds. You can place more than one kind of herb in a pot if the pot is large and wide. Or keep smaller, separate pots for each type of herb.

Place your container in a sunny place, and keep the soil moist. Soon you'll see small shoots popping up. As your herbs grow, some may take over. If the oregano bullies out the dill, remember to give it its own pot next time!

HERB GARDEN POTATO SALAD

Herbs are easy to grow in backyard gardens, pots on the patio, or windowsill gardens. Just snip off what you need and toss it into this easy, summery side dish. Adding the zest of a lemon brightens the flavor. Zest is the yellow part of a lemon peel, so it's extra important to use an organic lemon, with pesticide-free skin!

Ingredients*

2 pounds small potatoes (red, white, or purple)

4 tablespoons olive oil

1 tablespoon balsamic vinegar

fresh herbs, including chives, thyme, sage, parsley, dill, and basil, about ½ tablespoon of each, chopped

½ teaspoon lemon zest

salt and pepper to taste

* Look for organic versions of these ingredients when possible.

Steps

Wash and scrub the potatoes to remove any dirt. Place the potatoes in a saucepot and just cover the potatoes with water.

Cover and heat on high until boiling. Then turn the heat down to medium-low. Simmer for about 15 to 20 minutes, until potatoes are tender.

Drain the potatoes in a colander and let cool. Cut into bite-sized cubes.

To make the dressing, whisk together the oil, vinegar, herbs, lemon zest, salt, and pepper in a large bowl.

Add the potatoes to the bowl. Toss gently with a spoon until the potatoes are well coated.

CHAPTER FIVE

STRAIGHT FROM THE SOURCE

MICHAEL POLLAN, IN HIS BOOK *THE OMNIVORE'S DILEMMA*, DISCUSSES THE IMPORTANCE OF KNOWING THE SOURCE OF YOUR FOOD. "The organic label itself—like every other such label in the supermarket—is really just an imperfect substitute for direct observation of how a food is produced," he said. In other words, the best way to know if something's organic is to know more about how it's processed. That might be easy if you buy your food locally. For example, if you buy your eggs from a neighbor, you might even see the chickens that laid them. If you pick your apples at an orchard, you can ask the owner about his choice of pesticides. But it can be hard to track down the sources of all of your food.

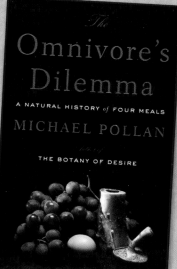

CHECK THEM OUT!

Most organic practices are easier on a smaller scale, on a farm with fewer acres and livestock. When your food comes from a large company, you may have to trust that their organic claims are true. Some large organic companies may have just jumped on the organic bus because it's a popular trend. While they may follow all of the organic regulations, they may still feed their cows an unnatural diet of corn, or keep their animals in crowded conditions. If you want to know more about an organic company, research it on the Internet. Companies often state their overall mission on their websites.

Stonyfield Farm, for example, has made organic a priority. The world's largest organic yogurt company gets its milk and other ingredients from organic farms that do not use synthetic pesticides or fertilizers, growth hormones, or antibiotics. They've gone beyond the government regulationst by making sure their delivery trucks are full, by using renewable energy sources at the factory, and by reducing, reusing, and recycling their waste.

Larger organic companies also help spread the word. A smaller organic farm can only serve a limited community. Products from a big company have distribution throughout the country. This helps share the organic message with a wider audience.

Organic companies often go beyond the farm to conserve resources. Stonyfield Farm uses renewable solar power to generate some of the electricity used in its yogurt factory.

Certified Organic Cropland and Pasture/Rangeland from 2000 to 2008 [in millions of acres]

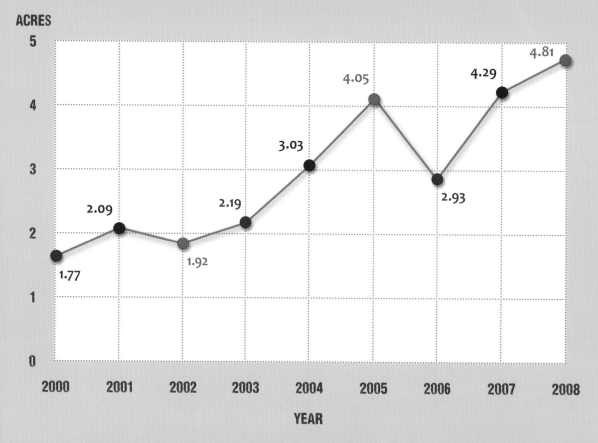

ACRES

5

4

3

2

1

0

2000 — 1.77
2001 — 2.09
2002 — 1.92
2003 — 2.19
2004 — 3.03
2005 — 4.05
2006 — 2.93
2007 — 4.29
2008 — 4.81

YEAR

Another way to check up on the source, and have fun with family or friends at the same time, is to take a tour of a food company. Large companies sometimes hold tours of their facilities so you can see the process up close. You can tour smaller, local companies too. If you live in the Northeast, you might be able to visit an organic maple sugaring operation. Watch the trees being tapped, see the machines they use to make the syrup, and even try a sample.

USE YOUR VOICE

Maybe while you're enjoying an organic homemade cookie, your friend is scarfing down a whole box of packaged nonorganic ones. Will your food choices really make a difference to help the planet?

Your friends will see you've switched. They'll ask you why. You can share your concerns with them. The next time those friends are shopping with their family, they might suggest Mom, Dad, or Grandma try organic. Word will spread.

Stores will notice that they are selling more organic products. So they'll keep more in stock. The organic companies that make those products will grow. Other companies will see that success, and think about going organic too!

Your plate is powerful. Make your voice heard.

WILL WORK FOR FOOD

Farmers Mark and Joanie run Wild Carrot Farm, in Canton, Connecticut. They are certified organic—and it's a lot of work. They weed by hand or with a cultivating tractor. They compost leaves, manure, grass clippings, and old produce. They rotate their crops from field to field so they are less susceptible to disease. They plant an extra "cover crop" in the fall after the harvest. This crop dries out and gets tilled into the fields in the spring to renew the soil's nutrients.

In 2008 the USDA reported more than 4.8 million acres of certified organic cropland and pastures. This is only about 0.6 percent of total farmland in the United States.

Besides being organic, Wild Carrot is also a CSA farm—CSA stands for Community Supported Agriculture. CSA farms sell "shares" of their business to customers. That means the customers pay ahead of time, before the growing season. This money helps Mark and Joanie buy the organic seeds, potting soil, compost, plastic trays, and irrigation supplies to get their crops started in the greenhouse. It helps them hire the early labor needed to plant the crops on their leased 10 acres. Then, at harvest time, those customers visit the farm store to pick up their produce.

Customers can also buy a work share. They don't buy it with money. Instead, they agree to work for a certain number of hours at the farm during the year. In exchange, they get credit to buy produce.

That's what Arlee and Clay's family did. These 11-year-old twins and their mom decided to do a work share at Wild Carrot. Arlee helped plant a potato field on the back of a transplanter pulled by a big tractor. She planted leeks and tomatoes and picked raspberries. Throughout the hot summer, "I watered a lot!" she says. Clay lifted 75-pound bags of corn, mowed the lawn, and restocked shelves. They both helped their mother in the farm store when there wasn't other work to do, assisting customers and fixing displays.

Working on a Community Supported Agriculture farm can be a great learning experience for the whole family.

Compost

The Richest Soil in Town!

Some organic gardeners and farmers avoid buying fertilizer by making their own compost. Composting is a type of recycling—but not the plastic bottles or metal cans from the recycling bin. Composting recycles organic material. In this case organic means "natural" trash that contains carbon and nitrogen—the nutrients plants need.

The best soil for plants contains a lot of decayed organic material. In nature, bacteria, microbes, and earthworms "eat" organic matter and cause it to decay into humus (the organic part of soil). Composting helps this process along. The result is nutrient-rich soil to use in your backyard or container garden.

Carbon can be found in brown organic yard waste, such as fallen dry leaves, wood chips, straw, and sawdust. Brown waste also includes newspaper and cardboard. You can even toss in a toilet paper roll, egg carton, or cereal box. (Just avoid cardboards that are coated in plastic.) Nitrogen is found in green waste, such as grass clippings, weeds, and raw fruit and vegetable scraps from your kitchen, such as apple cores, potato skins, and celery ends.

Compost can be kept in a pile or a composting bin. Layer about an equal amount of "browns" and "greens," watering after each layer. Cover it with a tarp or lid. About once or twice a week, turn the pile over, to get some of the bottom material to the top. This cools off the pile (all those microbes generate heat). Keep the pile moist, but not soggy.

When the compost has turned into rich, dark humus and you no longer see bits of your scraps, mix it up with the soil in your garden. If you feed those microbes what they want, they'll feed you back with nutritious produce!

On an organic farm, a little hard work brings rewards for your taste buds and the planet.

Even though the work was sometimes hard—such as bringing the very heavy zucchinis for storage in the coolers overnight—it opened their eyes to something new. "Before I worked there," Arlee says, "I didn't think much about eating healthy." Clay didn't realize how much work went into getting vegetables from the farm to his table.

Farmers Mark and Joanie are pleased with the community support. "Part of our mission is to teach kids," Joanie says, "not just about eating healthy but about learning together to be part of a community."

Organic is good for the planet. It's good for your body.

It brings people together too.

PICK-YOUR-OWN CRUMBLE

During the year local farms and orchards post "pick-your-own" signs. Pick your favorites to make this organic crumble.

Ingredients*

4 cups freshly picked fruit, such as apples, pears, peaches, strawberries, blueberries, or blackberries (alone or combined, as desired)

¼ cup sugar

½ teaspoon cinnamon

2 tablespoons white flour

3 tablespoons chilled butter

⅓ cup whole wheat flour

⅓ cup packed brown sugar

¼ cup oats

* Look for organic versions of these ingredients when possible.

Steps

Preheat oven to 375°F.

If you are using apples, pears, or peaches, peel off the skins and slice into pieces. If you are using berries, wash and pat dry. Place your fruit in a bowl.

Add the sugar, cinnamon, and white flour. Stir gently with a spoon so the fruit is well covered. Pour into an 8x8 inch baking pan.

In another bowl, combine the butter, whole wheat flour, brown sugar, and oats. Squeeze the mixture with your hands to distribute the butter until the mixture is crumbly. Sprinkle over the fruit to create a "crust."

Bake for about 35 to 40 minutes, until the crumble is nicely browned and fruit is bubbly.

Let cool for about 10 minutes.

METRIC CONVERSIONS

TEMPERATURE

degrees Fahrenheit	degrees Celsius
250	120
300	150
350	180
375	190
400	200
425	220

WEIGHT

United States	Metric
1 ounce	30 grams
½ pound	225 grams
1 pound	455 grams
10 pounds	4.5 kilograms

VOLUME

United States	Metric
¼ teaspoon	1.2 milliliters
½ teaspoon	2.5 milliliters
1 teaspoon	5 milliliters
1 tablespoon	15 milliliters
¼ cup	60 milliliters
⅓ cup	80 milliliters
½ cup	120 milliliters
1 cup	240 milliliters
1 quart	1 liter

AREA

United States	Metric
1 acre	0.4 hectare

GLOSSARY

biocontrol using natural enemies to control pests

compost decaying natural matter that is used to fertilize soil

efficient performing the best with the least amount of cost

feces solid waste from animals

groundwater water found in underground chambers; it is tapped for drinking water through wells and springs

humus the organic part of soil

invasive tending to spread quickly and harmfully; often occurs when a species is introduced to an environment where it doesn't occur naturally

irradiation exposure to light rays that kill bacteria

native natural to an area

nutrient a substance in food that a body needs to grow and function

organic processed in a more natural way to help conserve the health of land, animals, and crops

pesticide a chemical used to kill insects or small animals

subsidy monetary aid given to an industry to help with costs

sustainable a farming method that avoids waste, pollution, or damage to the environment

synthetic artificial, not natural

till to plow the land to break up the solid soil

READ MORE

Bijlefeld, Marjolijn, and Sharon K. Zoumbaris. *Food and You: A Guide to Healthy Habits for Teens.* Westport, Conn: Greenwood Press, 2008.

Gold, Rozanne. *Eat Fresh Food: Awesome Recipes for Teen Chefs.* New York: Bloomsbury Children's Books, 2009.

Pollan, Michael. *Food Rules: An Eater's Manual.* New York: Penguin Books, 2009.

Pollan, Michael. *The Omnivore's Dilemma, Young Reader's Edition: The Secrets Behind What You Eat.* New York: Dial, 2009.

INTERNET SITES

Use *FactHound* to find Internet sites related to this book. All of the sites on *FactHound* have been researched by our staff.

Here's all you do:

Visit *www.facthound.com*

Type in this code: **9780756545239**

ABOUT THE AUTHOR

Dana Meachen Rau has written more than 300 books for children and teens, including cookbooks that encourage healthy, thoughtful eating. She visits farm stands, tends her garden, and makes meals with her family in Burlington, Connecticut.

INDEX